The Eye of an Ant

The Eye of an Ant

Persian Proverbs & Poems
rendered into English Verse

by
Fatollah Akbar

IRANBOOKS
Bethesda, Maryland

The Eye of an Ant
Persian Proverbs and Poems
rendered into English Verse
by Fatollah Akbar

Copyright © 1995 Fatollah Akbar

ISBN 0-936347-56-2

Manufactured in the United States of America

The paper used in this book meets the minimum
requirements of the American National Standard for
Information Services–Permanence of Paper for
Printed Library Materials, ANSI Z39.48-1984

Iranbooks, Inc.
6831 Wisconsin Avenue
Bethesda, Maryland 20815 USA
Telephone: (301)986-0079
Facsimile: (301)907-8707

Library of Congress Cataloging-in-Publication Data

Akbar, Fatollah, 1940-
The Eye of an ant : Persian proverbs & poems
rendered into English verse / by Fatollah Akbar.
p. cm.
ISBN 0-936347-56-2 (alk. paper)
1. Proverbs, Persian. 2. Proverbs, Persian--
Translations into English. 3. Persian poetry.
4. Persian poetry--Translations into English. I. Title.
PN6519.P5A43 1995
398.9'9155--dc20 94-48744
CIP

This work is dedicated to all those
who cultivate the Persian language
and culture.

PREFACE

During my adolescence, I began to develop a substantial interest in the art of poetry, both in English and in my native tongue, Persian. As the years went by this interest became an obsession. However, it was not until the late seventies, at the age of thirty-nine, that I attained the urge and desire to write my own poetry. Due to the fact that I had been educated in Britain and the United States, I found it easier to write my poems in English.

In 1992, I embarked on a new form of literary undertaking — combining the two different cultures of my background in a single medium. This is how this work came to be. Specifically, I have attempted to provide my own English translation of some of the works of the great Persian poets such as Ferdowsi, Sa'di, Rumi and Hafez. Included in the translations are also prose excerpts of other Persian writers, some well-known and some anonymous, as well as a number of proverbs, witticisms and folk-sayings from my homeland.

The 282 versified pieces that are here presented are not literal translations; nonetheless they are faithful to the meaning and the spirit of the originals. I am hoping that my modest endeavor will benefit English-speaking readers and show them a glimpse of Persian wisdom as it is reflected in her poetry and proverbs. I trust that Persian youth and the offspring of Iranians who are away from their land of birth will find it of assistance in acquainting themselves further with the rich culture of Iran. To this end the original Persian is also included. Wherever possible, the original author has been identified.

ACKNOWLEDGMENTS

I am honored to have such prominent scholars as Ehsan Yarshater and M.J. Mahjoub offer their helpful insights. I am also sincerely appreciative of their encouragement.

Mr. Khosro Eghbal has been as always a key figure in my life. I am deeply grateful to him.

Three years ago my sister Goli Kashani encouraged me to share my poems with others and to publish them. I would like to thank her for her valuable effort and contribution in assisting me to prepare my manuscript. Above all, she has been the inspiration for bringing this idea to fruition.

I find it also appropriate and relevant to extend my sincere gratitude to Gilan Tocco Corn, my other dear sister, who has never failed to comfort and support me.

And finally I wish to express my appreciation to my dear mother, Fahimé Akbar for her patience and her unflagging confidence in me.

- 1 -

Able be the one, whose wisdom is truthful
For in wisdom lies the heart that is youthful
— *Ferdowsi*

توانا بود هر که دانا بود
ز دانش دل پیر برنا بود

. . . .

- 2 -

Never harm an ant that drags a seed
For it too has life, and loves it indeed
— *Ferdowsi*

میازار موری که دانه‌کش است
که جان دارد و جان شیرین خوش است

. . . .

- 3 -

Set pace to toil; never question its perception
For the gain is eternal; far from deception
— *Bahar*

برو کار میکن مگو چیست کار
که سرمایه جاودانی است کار

. . . .

- 4 -

Our intake of food continuously prevails
Beware of the time, whereupon harvest thus fails
— *Sa'di*

تنور شـکم دم بدم تافتن
مصیبت بود روز نایافتن

. . . .

- 5 -

We, the children of Adam, are components of one body
Created by an essence so truthfully great
Should agony strike one certain part of the body
Other parts would be reflected, by this pain-staking fate
If one cares not of the other person's grief
His life would be in shambles, for his happiness is Brief
— *Sa'di*

بنی آدم اعضـای یکدیگرند
که در آفرینش ز یک گوهرند
چو عضوی بدرد آورد روزگار
دگــر عضـوها را نـماند قرار
تو کز محنت دیگران بی غمی
نشاید که نـامت نهند آدمی

. . . .

Once when you have all the riches a
Everyone becomes your brother, and

اگر تو را زر باشد

عالمی تو را برادر باشد

. . . .

Come up with the capital if you will
And I'll make an effort with my skill

از شما عباسی، از من رقاصی

. . . .

Imposing on someone for a loan
Decreases the dignity that you own

از کیسه کسی قرض مکن

. . . .

Beets never turn to meat
Foes never treat you sweet

چغندر گوشت نمیشه، دشمن دوست نمیشه

. . . .

- 10 -

Down the lowest level, he feels a disgrace
Right on top of it all, that's just not his place

پائین پائین‌ها جایش نیست
بالا   بالاها   راهش نیست

. . . .

- 11 -

You might be looking very neat
In a posh imperial suite
But still to me you're valueless
Far from eloquence and elite

اگر بپوشی رختی، بنشینی به تختی
تازه می‌بینمت به چشم آن وقتی

. . . .

- 12 -

He feasts with a pack of hungry wolves
Whose fury runs real deep
He grieves with the desperate shepherd
Over the loss of a sheep

با گرگ دنبه میخوره، با چوپان گریه می‌کنه

. . . .

- 13 -

When it's torn
It can't be worn

چیزی که شده پاره، وصله ور نمیداره

. . . .

- 14 -

A thorn he well sees in other peoples' eyes
Yet it's the arrow in his own that he denies

خار را در چشم دیگران می‌بیند و تیر را در چشم خود نه

. . . .

- 15 -

A house with housewives that are double
Nuisance tends to make much trouble

خانه‌ای که دو کدبانوست، خاک تا زانوست

. . . .

- 16 -

God is so compassionate, yet She is so strict
Her fury is boundless, when a weakling is tricked

خدا دیر گیره، اما سخت گیره

. . . .

- 17 -

To bring about some laughter
Requires a happy heart
Alas, when you are sad with tears
Your eyes thus play a part

خنده کردن دل خوش می‌خواهد، گریه کردن سر و چشم

- 18 -

In an attempt to beautify her brows
Before she went ahead
She made a careless, big mistake
Which blinded her instead

خواست زیر ابروشو برداره، چشمشو کور کرد

- 19 -

The ass is still the ass, who often makes the rattle
He's always to be recognized, even in a new saddle

خر همان خره، پالانش عوض شده

- 20 -

Well spoken people are always safe and sound,
So never use a crooked tongue
For the words may spread around

خوش زبان باش، در امان باش

. . . .

- 21 -

This is done and I'm to blame
Therefore, know that I'm in shame

خودم کردم که لعنت بر خودم باد

. . . .

- 22 -

His humorless jokes are to him so amusing
It's his artistic touch that he seems to be losing

خود گوئی خود خندی
عجب مرد هنرمندی

. . . .

- *23* -

I once owned a fortune
But the past will never count
How good it is to accept me
With my humble amount

داشتم داشتم حساب نیست، دارم دارم حسابه

. . . .

- *24* -

You might weep for a little while
But see what will happen after
Tears will surely fade away
Bringing joy and laughter

— *Rumi*

در پس هر گریه، آخر خنده‌ایست

. . . .

- *25* -

Lock your house doors; latch your gate
Your neighbors, don't incriminate

در خانه را ببند، همسایه‌ات را دزد مکن

. . . .

- 26 -

When one should face an intruding guest
No one expects you to do your best

در خانه هر چه مهمان هر که
(وقتی مهمان سرزده برسد تکلیفی نیست)

. . . .

- 27 -

A tree so proud with loads of fruit
Can fall victim to an act of brute

درخت پربار، سنگ میخوره

. . . .

- 28 -

I do have problems, which to me are pain
Why should I listen, as my neighbors complain

درد دل خودم کم بود، اینهم قرقر همسایه

. . . .

- 29 -

All I do is sleep and eat
For God will keep me on my feet

بخور و بخواب کار منه، خدا نگهدار منه

. . . .

- 30 -

If infamy is what you hate
Join the crowd, don't hesitate

خواهی نشوی رسوا، همرنگ جماعت شو

. . . .

- 31 -

Picture life as a roller coaster
It has its ups and downs
You go and build it with success
Then suddenly destiny frowns

در همیشه بیک پاشنه نمیگرده، دنیا سرازیر و سربالا داره

. . . .

- 32 -

Forgiveness has its own delight
Where vengeance always proves its plight

در عفو لذتیست که در انتقام نیست

. . . .

- *33* -

A fool as a friend is a pest indeed
A foe that is wise could be blessed indeed
— *Nezami*

دشمن دانا به از نادان دوست

. . . .

- *34* -

The world as we know; is a place of testing
It focuses on hardship; rarely for resting

دنیا جای آزمایش نه جای آسایش

. . . .

- *35* -

One who boasts, that has friends alot
In the time of need, those friends are not

دوست همه کس دوست هیچکس نیست

. . . .

- *36* -

He's eager to find fault in others
To notice his own, he never bothers

دیگ به دیگ میگه روت سیاه

. . . .

- 37 -

Tales have been told about sisters-in-law
Relationships among them is nothing but raw

رخت دو جاری را در یک طشت نمیشه شست

. . . .

- 38 -

I went and did a good deed, but had a tough break
For instead of praises, I was burnt at the stake

رفتم ثواب کنم، کباب شدم

. . . .

- 39 -

I dropped to see my dear old aunt
To open my poor heart
But she herself had problems
Sorrowful from the start

رفتم خونه خاله دلم واشه، خاله خسید دلم پوسید

. . . .

- 40 -

The rhythm of her dancing, didn't cope with the song
So she claimed, that the platform was crooked all along

رقاصه نمی‌توانست برقصه گفت زمین کجه

. . . .

- 41 -

He, who without a tongue can't express his views
Is favored to the one, whose tongue is to abuse
— *Sa'di*

زبان بریده بکنجی نشسته صم بکم
به از کسی که نباشد زبانش اندر حکم

. . . .

- 42 -

If you give someone a hard smack
Expect another to strike you back

زدی ضربتی، ضربتی نوش کن

. . . .

- 43 -

A happy fruitful year
Is attributed to its Spring
May every year be fruitful
To every living thing

سالی که نکوست، از بهارش پیداست

. . . .

- 44 -

Beware of all gossipers
Whose intentions are to hurt
They stab you in the back with lies
But in front of you they flirt

آنکه پیش تو پشت سر دیگران بدگوئی میکند،
بدون شک پیش دیگران پشت سر تو بد خواهد گفت

. . . .

- 45 -

Although he's wrinkled and he's aged
Alas to a young girl he's engaged

سر پیری معرکه گیری

. . . .

- 46 -

The suitors are all fighting
Over the love of their queen
But the bride-to-be has no interest,
For her happiness is unseen

سرش جنگه، اما دلش تنگه

. . . .

- 47 -

No matter how sweet the honey may be
Vinegar is much sweeter, when offered free

سرکه مفت از عسل شیرین‌تره

. . . .

- 48 -

I don't want your prayers
When I'm laid to rest
Just keep the graveyard nice and clean
That is my request

در قبرم کثافت نکن، از فاتحه خواندنت گذشتم

. . . .

- 49 -

A hand that has no building skill
That hand could be the beggar's thrill

دست بی‌هنر کفچهٔ گدائی است

- 50 -

The world may overflow,
From a devastating flood
But he continues sleeping
No tension in his blood

دنیا را آب ببره، او را خواب میبره

- 51 -

A wound sustained from a tongue so malicious
is far worse, than a wound from a sword that is Vicious

زخم زبان از زخم شمشیر بدتر است

- 52 -

He's quite distinguished; well refined
Accomplishes things with his brilliant mind

سرش به کلاش میارزه

. . . .

- 53 -

Troubles are abundant, but lay off the search
For miseries in life, would leave you in the lurch

بیهوده برای خودت ایجاد زحمت نکن و به دنبال دردسر مرو

. . . .

- 54 -

A dog that is happy with a bone for a treat
Never harms its master, whose gesture's sweet

سگ پاچه صاحبش را نمیگیره

. . . .

- 55 -

A rider cannot visualize
The stance of a man on foot
The well-fed about the hungry
He cannot clearly put

سوار از پیاده خبر نداره
سیر از گرسنه خبر نداره

- 56 -

A firm and quick transaction
Could be rougher than a slap
But the one that is on credit
May be sweet and yet a trap

سیلی نقدی به از حلوای نسیه

- 57 -

It has always been recalled
That a comb is no use to the bald

کچل و شونه؟

- 58 -

If partners were good as a guide
God would have one by his side

شریک اگر خوب بود، خدا هم شریک میداشت

. . . .

- 59 -

The garden that has the jackal offended
Would profit the gardener, and everything is mended

شغالی که از باغ قهر کنه، باغبونه منفعت میکنه

. . . .

- 60 -

Listen well to what you've heard
But don't go believing every word

شنونده باید عاقل باشد

. . . .

- 61 -

In helping your loved ones
If you do refrain
The burden you'll carry
Will inflict you with pain

سر که نه در راه عزیزان بود، بار گرانی است کشیدن بدوش

. . . .

- 62 -

His shadow regretfully we came across
It's that shadow, that dragged us to our loss

صابونش به جامه ما خورده

. . . .

- 63 -

Hundreds of workers on the job
But the chores are far from finished
The fact is simply indolence
For their willingness to work has diminished

صدتا آدم تنبل اگر به کاری بپردازند نتیجه کم است

. . . .

- 64 -

The peacock's beauty is so amazing
Its royal design has everyone gazing
Yet the peacock itself is in full gloom
Thinks that its legs are not worth praising
— *Sa'di*

طاوسی را به نقش و نگاری که هست
خلق تحسین کنند و او خجل از پای از زشت خویش

. . . .

- 65 -

Dice that always hit the spot
Tend to make the players hot
Gamblers make the lucky shot
So they are the players, are they not?

طاس اگر نیک نشیند همه کس نراد است

. . . .

- 66 -

The drum is so noisy, but there's nothing within it
Like a loud shallow speaker, who bores you each minute

طبل توخالی است

. . . .

- 67 -

A doctor who's ruthless, is a curse to each nation
He wants to see the sickness, of God's mass creation

طبیب بی‌مروت خلق را رنجور میخواهد

- 68 -

Family ties become depleted
By tyrants who are self-conceited

ظالم همیشه خانه خراب است

- 69 -

With saints he appears to be on one level
In reality however he has signed with the devil

خوش ظاهر و بد باطن

- 70 -

A heart so agonizing, reflects the love that starts
And the gravest illness ever, is the malady of hearts
— *Rumi*

عاشقی پیداست از زاری دل
نیست بیماری چو بیماری دل

. . . .

- 71 -

A scholar with no practice, who is reluctant to strive
Is like an idle bee, at a honeyless hive
— *Sa'di*

عامل بی عمل، زنبور بی عسله

. . . .

- 72 -

It is simply easy, to bring oneself to learn
But to qualify as a human, it is hard to earn

ملا شدن چه آسون، آدم شدن چه مشکل

. . . .

- 73 -

How clever is the way of love, that captures every Hour
Endurance of all misfortunes, is formed by this power

— *Hafez*

عاشقی شیوه رندان بلاکش باشد

- 74 -

A searcher must command his mind
With abundant effort he will find

— *Rumi*

عاقبت جوینده یابنده است

- 75 -

While the wise man was debating
As to how to cross the stream
The fool jumped in and walked across
And smiled back with a gleam

عاقل بکنار آب تا پل میجست، دیوانه پابرهنه از آب گذشت

- 76 -

Committing an act with incredible haste
Is the job of the Satan at his finest taste

عجله کار شیطان است

. . . .

- 77 -

What predicament is one in
When one's excuse is worse than sin

عذر بدتر از گناه

. . . .

- 78 -

The bride is young and the groom is old
Sarcastic tales of this are told

طعنه به مرد که با زن جوان ازدواج کرد

. . . .

- 79 -

The night the bride was to be mine
The hours had started to decline

عروس که بما رسید شب کوتاه شد

. . . .

- 80 -

The bride is not so pretty
She looks so pale and thin
But don't blame the mother-in-law
For the poor ordeal she's in

عروس مردنی را گردن مادر شوهر نگذار

. . . .

- 81 -

Devotion to the people
And saving their utmost needs
Is better than just praying
With fancy gowns and beads

— *Sa'di*

عبادت بجز خدمت خلق نیست
به تسبیح و سجاده و دلق نیست

. . . .

- 82 -

If there is no mind at work
A tender life will go berserk

عقل که نیست جون در عذابه

. . . .

- 83 -

Prior to the incident, come up with the cure
Otherwise the aftermath, is difficult to endure

علاج واقعه پیش از وقوع باید کرد

. . . .

- 84 -

He's unemployed and idle
But his pastime is amazing
He takes his goose, and turns it loose
And watches as it's grazing

غاز میچرونه

. . . .

- 85 -

The grief of the death of a brother
Is known by the sibling and none other

غم مرگ برادر را برادر مرده میداند

. . . .

- 86 -

When upon us bloweth the wind of Autumn
That nature has empowered
Then it shall come to perfect view
the sign of the brave and the coward
— *Ebn Yamin*

فردا که بر من و تو وزد باد مهرگان
آنگه شود پدید که نامرد و مرد کیست

· · · · · · · · · · · · · · · · · · · ·

- 87 -

An offspring with no manners, is like an awkward hand
The hand displays six fingers, one more than actually
Planned If the finger is disposed of, how painful it will be
But if you let it stay right there It's ugly, you can see

فرزند بی‌ادب مثل انگشت ششم است،
اگر ببری درد میگیره، اگر نبری زشت است

· · · · · · · · · · · · · · · · · · · ·

- 88 -

A nosy person plunged into hell
But he was nosy there as well

فضول در همه جا فضول است،
فضول را بردند جهنم، گفت هیزمش تره

· · · · · · · · · · · · · · · · · · · ·

- 89 -

Pepper may be small in size
But it's power's hot, and burns your eyes

فلفل نبین چه ریزه، بشکن ببین چه تیزه

. . . .

- 90 -

The ground remains his carpet
And his blanket is the sky
The man is surely penniless
So how can he get by

فرشش زمینه، لحافش آسمون
(آه در بساط نداره)

. . . .

- 91 -

Now that you're in times of peace
Think of your armament growing
It's too late to build a dam
When already the flood is flowing

بروزگار سلامت سلاح جنگ بساز،
وگرنه سیل چو بگرفت سد نشاید بست

. . . .

- 92 -

It's been proven, many a time
The killer returns to the scene of the crime

قاتل به پای خود پای دار میره

. . . .

- 93 -

Go and finish your little chore
Stressful jobs are asked no more

کار کوچک را انجام بده، کار بزرگ از تو نخواستیم

. . . .

- 94 -

If you should to economize
Your wealth and power would surely rise
— *Sa'di*

قناعت توانگر کند مرد را

. . . .

- 95 -

One who experiences a tragic event
Will appreciate what his happiness meant
— *Sa'di*

قدر عافیت کسی داند که به مصیبتی گرفتار آید

. . . .

- 96 -

Put your effort to what you do
Accuracy is a factor too

کار از محکم کاری عیب نمیکنه

. . . .

- 97 -

We know that carpentry is a trade
Indeed for monkeys, it's not made

کار بوزینه نیست نجاری

. . . .

- 98 -

Don't approach us, it's no use
"I can't do this;" is no excuse

کار نشد ندارد

. . . .

- 99 -

Whatever one's achievements are
Justice and fairness are linked by far

کار بکن بهر ثواب، نه سیخ بسوزه نه کباب

(باید جانب انصاف را رعایت کرد)

. . . .

- 100 -

If only the sweetness of life would prevail
If only our goodness to others would not fail
But the seed is hard to cultivate
If only in destiny we would not trail

کاشکی را کاشتند سبز نشد

. . . .

- 101 -

The bowl is hotter than the soup
A situation is in a loop

کاسه گرمتر از آش

. . . .

- 102 -

Behold of a pen in the hand of a foe
Where wicked scripts will come to show

قلم دست دشمنه

. . . .

- 103 -

Whatever you tell me, I believe in full
For the habit of swearing is against my rule

قسم نخور که باور کردم

. . . .

- 104 -

Debts do reach a large proportion
A trend you might not yearn
But once it's there, have no despair
and show your least concern

قرض که رسید به صد تومان بی‌خیال باش

. . . .

- 105 -

Should I take your word for not being a thief
or the tail of the missing rooster should I believe

قسمت را باور کنم یا دم خروس را

. . . .

- 106 -

The cat has no access to the meat
So the creature claims, it's foul to eat

گربه دستش بگوشت نمیرسه، میگه بوگند میده

. . . .

- 107 -

Wherever he desires, he rents a place
Therefore, he always has a smiling face

کرایه نشین خوش نشین است

. . . .

- 108 -

I demand of no one, to scratch my itching back
My finger nails are trying, to follow the right track

کس نخارد پشت من جز ناخن انگشت من

. . . .

- 109 -

A tree when decaying, as one can see
Is linked to the condition of the tree

کرم از خود درخته

. . . .

- 110 -

He, whose wife's sister had been deprived of life
Would never in his prayers, ask the death of his wife

کسی دعا میکند زنش بمیرد که خواهر زن داشته باشد

. . . .

- 111 -

Should this be a happy world, then what part is
Happiness is that part, where our heart is

کجا خوش است، آنجا که دل خوش است

. . . .

- 112 -

He's eloquent in all his speeches
But his message adversely reaches

خوب حرف میزند، ولی حرف خوب نمیزند

. . . .

- 113 -

He, who during youthful years,
Had never made a name
Later, when he's old and gray,
He'll never reach his aim

کسی که در جوانی به جائی نرسید در پیری نخواهد رسید

. . . .

- 114 -

He acts like a rooster that freely crows
He seems to be cheerful, and that's how it shows

کبکش خروس میخونه

. . . .

- 115 -

The spatula has reached to the bottom of the pot
There is no more left and he's a have-not

کفگیرش به ته دیگ خورده
(آه در بساط نداره)

. . . .

- 116 -

When approached by a wolf, he becomes frightful
So for him to guard a herd, is not quite rightful

کسی که از گرگ می‌ترسه، نباید گوسفند نگه‌داره

. . . .

- 117 -

Never go hungry, yet never be full
Eat in moderation; that's the rule

کم بخور، همیشه بخور

. . . .

- 118 -

The few words that are spoken clearly
Are to many valued dearly

کم بگو، سنجیده گو

. . . .

- 119 -

An evening of glamour, at a certain ball
Are the blind pleased at this at all?

کور را چه به شب نشینی

. . . .

- 120 -

Freshness of all sorts
That your tender heart pleases
Yet sadly their period
So rapidly ceases

هر چیز تازه مدتی کوتاه دلچسب و دل پذیر است

. . . .

- 121 -

We do wholeheartedly receive our guests
But if they stay long, they become pests

کنگر خورده، لنگر انداخته

. . . .

- 122 -

Mountains never reach each other
But human beings do
At times of hardship and despair
they reach out to you

کوه به کوه نمیرسه آدم به آدم میرسه

. . . .

- 123 -

He lost his job in a freak event
Imagine what to him this meant

گاوش زائید

. . . .

- 124 -

He built a reputation
As a server to mankind
But then he made a grave mistake
And his state was undermined

کسی که خدمت میکند و با کوچکترین
آزار خدمت خودرا پایمال میکند
(گاو نه من شیر)

. . . .

- 125 -

He's so stubborn, and adds such a grudge
You ask him to move, but he's reluctant to budge

یک دنده و لجوج

. . . .

- 126 -

If drunks are legally to be caught
Then everyone to jail is brought

— *Rumi*

گر حکم شود که مست گیرند
در شهر هر آنچه هست گیرند

. . . .

- 127 -

You claim to be much better
Then why don't you give a try
Otherwise, don't criticize
Because all of this is a lie

— *Rumi*

گر تو بهتر میزنی، بستان بزن

. . . .

- 128 -

If embarking on a venture that aims for winning
You must be solid from the beginning

کار را باید از ابتدا محکم گرفت

. . . .

- 129 -

He, who boasts against the week
Against the stronger, he's frightened to speak
— *Sa'di*

گربه شیر است در گرفتن موش،
لیک موش است در مصاف پلنگ

. . . .

- 130 -

From excessive running
You wear out your shoes
Aside from a few pounds
That you tend to lose

از زیادی دویدن کفش پاره میشه، گر زمین و زمان بهم دوزی

. . . .

- 131 -

Put a little effort, and eliminate the strain
Result of which, will never be in vain

گره کز دست بگشاید به
چه آزاریست دندان را
(کار را باید آسان گرفت)

. . . .

- 132 -

In a street called reputation
My passage is forbidden
If one does not approve of this
My fate is overridden

— *Hafez*

در کوی نیکنامی ما را گذر ندادند،
گر تو نمی‌پسندی تغییر ده قضا را

. . . .

- 133 -

I dwell not, from the prominence of my father
But want to make a name of my own, much rather

گرد نام پدر چه میگردی، پدر خویش باش اگر مردی

. . . .

- 134 -

Snakes can be found where the treasure is
Thorns grow deep in the flowers
Grief is around where the pleasure is
Thus, hurting our fun loving hours

گنج بی مار و گل بی خار نیست
شادی بی غم در این بازار نیست

. . . .

- 135 -

Profits must be seized from the upper-class
Not from the destitute of the mass

گوشت را از بغل گاو باید برید،
منفعت را از پولدار باید برد نه از مردم بینوا

. . . .

- 136 -

We nourished daily from the wheat
Considered as a sin
Then vanished was the Paradise
That happily we were in

گندم خوردیم از بهشت بیرونمان کردند

. . . .

- 137 -

Rubies, pearls and emeralds and such
Have to be pure to mean so much
Not every stone one touches, is coral of the sea
Otherwise, imagine how wealthy one would be

گوهر پاک بباید که شود قابل فیض،
ورنه هر سنگ و گلی لؤلؤ و مرجان نشود

. . . .

- 138 -

They say he's well-experienced
And has been through a lot
An asset in his line of work
Placed in the right spot

گیسش را توی آسیاب سفید نکرده

. . . .

- 139 -

Advices that you give
For others to abide them
Why is it that you, yourself
Have never, ever tried them

لالائی میدونی چرا خوابت نمیبره؟
چرا نصیحت که بدیگران میکنی خودت عمل نمیکنی؟

. . . .

- 140 -

A great philosopher was once asked
From whom have you learned your good breeding?
From the ones who are rude with a raw attitude
Where good manners they sure must be needing
                              — *Sa'di*

لقمان را گفتند ادب را از که آموختی، گفت از بی‌ادبان

. . . .

- 141 -

We're on opposite borders
Which to me is fine
You tend to your business
And I shall tend to mine

ما این ور جوب تو آن ور جوب بکار هم کار نداریم

. . . .

- 142 -

A burnt heart of a mother, will make her hurt
While a nanny suffers only from a burning skirt

مادر را دل سوزد، دایه را دامان

. . . .

- 143 -

The stingy are not born to be kind
So erase this whole thought off your mind

ما را باش که از بز دنبه میخواهیم
(کنایه از انتظار محبت از شخص ممسک)

. . . .

- 144 -

A snake will dispose its colorful skin
But never the character it has within

مار پوست خودشو ول میکنه، اما خوی خودش را ول نمیکنه

. . . .

- 145 -

The Satan wonders why he's blamed
For a death from a simple dish
The victim made a grave mistake
Eating yogurt mixed with fish

ماهی و ماست عزرائیل میگه تقصیر ماست

. . . .

- 146 -

They look alike in every way
Their move, their voice, their laugh
Extraordinary, I must say
As an apple cut in half

مثل سیبی را که از وسط نصف کرده باشند

. . . .

- 147 -

With forty the man is in his prime
No wonder he's having the best of time

مرد چهل ساله تازه اول چلچلیشه

. . . .

- 148 -

How clever was the chicken
How cautious and real quick
But one day, a trap was set
The trap that did the trick

مرغ زیرک که میرمید از دام، با همه زیرکی بدام افتاد

. . . .

- 149 -

Enmity prevails between two guests
And the host assumes, that both are pests

مهمان مهمان را نمی تواند ببیند، صاحب خانه هر دو را

. . . .

- 150 -

A visitor could be dear to us
Yet similar to a breath;
When coming in, it won't go out
Will suffocate is to death

میهمان گر چه عزیز است ولیکن چو نفس،
خفه سازد که فرود آید و بیرون نرود

· · · · · · · · · · · · · · · · · ·

- 151 -

For visitors who are not expected
Accommodation makes no sense
So if they wish to see us
It'll be at their own expense

مهمان ناخونده خرجش پای خودشه

· · · · · · · · · · · · · · · · · ·

- 152 -

He, who claims illegally
To inherit the other's land
Is better than the parasite
Who pesters a generous hand

چشته خوار بدتر از میراث خوار است

· · · · · · · · · · · · · · · · · ·

- 153 -

It's been said that at a fight, a mouse alive
Is better than a cat that didn't survive

موش زنده بهتر از گربه مرده است

- 154 -

If all the blades in the world
Were rattling for the thrill
No veins would be slashed
Without God's will

اگر تیغ عالم بجنبد ز جای، نبرد رگی تا نخواهد خدای

- 155 -

You offer me goodies, to have me fed
Then all of a sudden, you smash my head

نخودچی تو جیبم میکنی، آنوقت سرم را میشکنی

- 156 -

He shows up at different scenes
In each affair, he intervenes

نخود همه آش
(کسی که در هر کاری دخالت میکند)

. . . .

- 157 -

He made a fortune overnight
Then bragged how much it cost
He might have earned a lot of things
But himself is what he lost

ندید و بدید وقتی بدید ز جا پرید
(کسانی که خودشان را گم میکنند وقتی بجائی میرسند)

. . . .

- 158 -

If step by step, the ladder you climb
You'll reach the very top in due time

نردبون پله پله

. . . .

- *159* -

This is the saying about the doors
Don't knock theirs, so they won't knock yours

نزن در کسی را تا نزند درت را

. . . .

- *160* -

In various jobs, you lack the skill
So to hire you, no one will

نکرده کار را نگیر به کار

. . . .

- *161* -

Bread and water, I get free
So this is the place I'd rather be

نون اینجا، آب اینجا، کجا بروم به از اینجا

. . . .

- *162* -

The bread is chewed for him to swallow
In learning facts, the man can't follow

نون را باید جوید و توی دهانش گذاشت

. . . .

- *163* -

I have neither strength
Nor powerful connection
Therefore, I am always known
As a victim of rejection

نه پشت دارم نه مشت

- *164* -

To drive a hard bargain
I have never tried
Yet I had been able
To bring in the bride

نه چک زدم نه چونه، عروس آمد تو خونه

- *165* -

I can't go forward, and I can't retreat
I can't get all my ends to meet

نه راه پس دارم نه راه پیش

- *166* -

I'm no head of an onion
I'm not even a core
I'm virtually a nobody
There's nothing I'm for

من نه سر پیازم نه ته پیاز

. . . .

- *167* -

Provide the people with bread and wheat
But the bread of some, refrain to eat

نون بهمه کس بده اما نون همه کس را نخور

. . . .

- *168* -

To purchase a donkey
Never send out the old
To bring in your bride
Pass up the young and the bold

نه پیررا برای خر خریدن بفرست،
نه جوان را برای زن گرفتن

. . . .

- 169 -

He's never known to blind one
As for a cure, he can't find one

نه کور میکنه، نه شفا میده

. . . .

- 170 -

One who has sustained a terrible loss
Is suspicious of others; even his boss

مارگزیده از ریسمان سیاه و سفید میترسه،
(شخص ضرر دیده همیشه نسبت بهمه ظنین است)

. . . .

- 171 -

A simple bowl of yogurt
Would put one's eyes to close
So set aside your daily work
For an hour to repose

ماست را خوردی کاسه اش را زیر سرت بگذار

. . . .

- *172* -

The breath of life is easy to perish
It is wealth that is sweet, that one has to cherish!

مال است نه جان است که آسان بتوان داد

. . . .

- *173* -

Fresh is the fish, as it struggles in the net
Never late are actions, whenever mind is set

ماهی را هر وقت از آب بگیری تازه است

. . . .

- *174* -

Death makes its visit
To all of us for sure
Whether we live in luxury
or whether we are poor

مرگ به فقیر و غنی نگاه نمیکند

. . . .

- 175 -

He just ate the donkey's brain
That's the reason he's insane

مغز خر خورده

- 176 -

Never make transactions
With a relative or friend
You'll find it quite deplorable
With a very bitter end

معامله با خودی غصه دارد

- 177 -

I speak of words of wisdom
Listen, as I stress my thought
You may follow my advice
Or be totally distraught

— Sa'di

من آنچه شرط بلاغ است با تو میگویم،
تو خواه از سخنم پند گیر و خواه ملال

- 178 -

Have no complaints from strangers,
For the cause of my ordeal
I blame the person whom I know
Who cares not how I feel

— *Hafez*

من از بیگانگان هرگز ننالم،
که با من هر چه کرد آن آشنا کرد

. . . .

- 179 -

I possess no fortune
For the court to confiscate
Neither do I have the faith
For the Devil to eliminate

نه مال دارم دیوان ببره
نه ایمان دارم شیطان ببره

. . . .

- 180 -

At dusk do not bow to pray
And add water to milk the following day

نه نماز شبگیر کن نه آب توی شیر کن

. . . .

- 181 -

The malice of a scorpion,
Whose sting stops short to kill
Has no connection to its wrath
It's the nature of its will

نیش عقرب نه از ره کین است،
اقتضای طبیعتش اینست

- 182 -

You're doing it freely, it's no task
So conclude the favor; do not ask

نیکی و پرسش

- 183 -

Goodness, Gracious!
It seems so odd
When a job is not performed by God

وای به کاری که نسازد خدا

- *184* -

It's so pathetic, is it not?
When a grain of salt begins to rot

وای به وقتی که بگندد نمک

. . . .

- *185* -

Oh! What a thought,
When a smuggler at large
Would work at the customs
And becomes in charge

وای به وقتی که قاچاقچی گمرکچی باشه

. . . .

- *186* -

In the midst of eating,
That delicious piece
The aunt does not recognize
Her nephew or niece

وقت خوردن خاله خواهرزاده را نمیشناسه

. . . .

- 187 -

He is a colonel when he gets his pay
And a soldier when he works all day

وقت مواجب سرهنگه، وقت کار کردن سربازه

. . . .

- 188 -

Every lowness has its height
This fact has been proven right

هر پستی بلندی داره

. . . .

- 189 -

Where there's a bear
One gets a scare

هر جا خرسه، جای ترسه

. . . .

- 190 -

Where there's a face of a fairy
There is also a demon so scary

هر جا پریرخی است دیو با اوست

. . . .

- 191 -

Be thankful for the salt you eat
At other people's table
Never destroy the salt dish
And make the grace unstable

هر جا که نمک خوری نمکدان نشکن

. . . .

- 192 -

What you disapprove for yourself, you see
Never approve for others, whatever the case may be

هر چه بخود نپسندی به دیگران نپسند

. . . .

- 193 -

Anywhere is nowhere
To reach your ultimate aim
But one right place, you'll surely face
The victory that you claim

هر جا هیچ جا یک جا همه جا

. . . .

- 194 -

The more the money
The more the stew
This proverb is old
Yet known to you

هر چه پول بدی آش میخوری

. . . .

- 195 -

Too bad that no one knew him
As a thief, a cheat and a crook
The truth remains, that he refrains
From giving back what he took

هر چه خورده پس نداده

. . . .

- 196 -

I can assure, that it's no mistake
The bigger the head; the greater the ache

هر چه سر بزرگتر درد بزرگتر

. . . .

- 197 -

Whatever was spinned, had turned to cotton
The fruit of our labor, we had never gotten

هر چه رشتیم پنبه شد
(کارمان بی نتیجه ماند)

. . . .

- 198 -

The good that you do onto others
As well as an evil deed
Will have an impact on yourself
There's no way you can impede

هر چه کنی بخود کنی گر همه نیک و بد کنی

. . . .

- 199 -

Whatever the outcome has in store
It's to our betterment, for less and more

هر چه پیش آید خوش آید

. . . .

- 200 -

I never owned a donkey
So I do not have a grief
The burden of its upkeep
Justifies my belief

من خری ندارم غمی ندارم

- 201 -

Each word that is uttered
Has its certain place
A point has its position
And yet has its space

هر سخن جائی و هر نکته مقامی دارد

- 202 -

Every night is a night of gratitude
If one is to have a worthful attitude

هر شب شب قدر است اگر قدر بدانی

- 203 -

If his hopes lie on the neighbor
To provide him with his meals
Then he'll go to sleep while starving
Now imagine how that feels

هر که به امید همسایه نشست، گرسنه میخوابه

. . . .

- 204 -

He, who has taken a disloyal stand
Tends to count with a trembling hand

هر که خیانت ورزد، دستش در حساب بلرزد

. . . .

- 205 -

In order to get to know one
To make acquaintance real
Make a journey with that man
Or close with him a deal

هر که را میخواهی بشناسی یا باهاش سفر کن یا معامله کن

. . . .

- 206 -

The mind of a person has always been planned
His work abiding colleague never to strand

همکار همکار را نمیتونه ببینه

. . . .

- 207 -

A neighbor who's close to where you are
Is better than a brother, who lives too far

همسایه نزدیک بهتر از برادر دور

. . . .

- 208 -

Clouds necessarily do not mean
A sprinkle of rain is to be seen

همه ابری بارون ندارد

. . . .

- 209 -

How frightful I may well appear
Yet my approach makes others fear

هم میترسم هم میترسانم

. . . .

- 210 -

Everything has a remedy
That is our perception
Death alone as we have known
Is by far an exception

همه چیز چاره داره، جز مرگ

. . . .

- 211 -

Since you indeed have given him birth
You have to raise him for what he's worth

همینو که زائیدی بزرگش کن

. . . .

- 212 -

His mouth still smells of baby milk
Namely he's immature
He claims he can accomplish things
Frankly one's not sure

دهنش بوی شیر میدهد

. . . .

- 213 -

There's always a reason for being cheap
Bear this in your mind to keep

هیچ ارزونی بی علت نیست

. . . .

- 214 -

A grocer retains his selling power
By never admitting, that his yogurt's sour

هیچ بقالی نمیگه ماست من ترشه

. . . .

- 215 -

A friend that betrays you
And proves to be fake
Is much worse than dealing
With a poisonous snake

— *Rumi*

یار بد بدتر بود از مار بد

. . . .

- 216 -

You either stay and work at home
Or in the streets you'll surely roam

یا کوچه گردی یا خانه دار

. . . .

- 217 -

They say that serpents hate pennyroyal
The mint that yields aromatic scent
Yet, for the snake it's quite a blow
When at its nest the pennyroyal grow

مار از پونه بدش می‌آید، در لونه‌اش سبز میشه

. . . .

- 218 -

The clearness of the spring that flows
Tarnished by the sight of dirt
Pollution stems from right at the top
Where the ones below get hurt

آب از سرچشمه گل است

. . . .

- 219 -

Whatever the fool may have to say
The madman believes him all the way

ابله گوید، دیوانه باور کند

- 220 -

They say that he, who tells a lie
His memory is dim
To delusion his fellow man
His chance is somewhat slim

آدم دروغگو کم حافظه میشه

- 221 -

A person who panics to get a job done
Has to start all over from square one

آدم دستپاچه کار را دوبار میکنه

- 222 -

The ear is a factor for the nurturing man
Whereas creatures become nurtured
By eating what they can

— *Rumi*

آدمی فربه شود از راه گوش
جانور فربه شود از نوش نوش

. . . .

- 223 -

No where is there for fire to know
Who's the friend and who's the foe

آتش دوست و دشمن نمیشناسه

. . . .

- 224 -

Through many moons preceding days
The farmer into the sky shall gaze
He counts the stars and so he waits
To gain the bread he cultivates

سال و مه در انتظار قرص نان،
شب تا صبح زارع چرا اخترشماری میکند

. . . .

- 225 -

Your simple step to gain success
Is the best of cause for God to bless

از تو حرکت، از خدا برکت

- 226 -

An offer of water, that given unexpected
Is totally desirable and well respected

آب نطلبیده مراد است

- 227 -

Those trees of willow that proudly grow
Are dauntless to the winds that blow

از آن بیدها نیست که از این بادها بلرزد

- 228 -

With the snap of your finger; in a flash
I'm all set; to you I dash

از تو بیک اشاره، از من بسر دویدن

- 229 -

Words that are spoken by a friend
Are sweet enough to inspire
A message from the intimate
Would lift one's spirit higher

از هر چه بگذری سخن دوست خوش‌تر است،
پیغام آشنا روح‌پرور است

. . . .

- 230 -

The words from Hell you tend to hear
Yet your touch of fire is far from near

از جهنم خبر میشنوی، دستی از دور بر آتش داری

. . . .

- 231 -

From God can nothing be concealed
To you my secret be revealed

از خدا پنهان نیست، از شما چه پنهان

. . . .

- 232 -

From limb to limb you keep on jumping
The actual facts, you keep on dumping

از این شاخ و آن شاخ

- 233 -

One would learn to be humble
With the worthiness of grace
Since downward flows the water
Alas, upward it can't race

افتادگی آموز اگر قابل فیضی،
هرگز نخورد آب زمینی که بلند است

- 234 -

Offspring whose parents
Have raised them so poorly
Alas, learn their lesson
For life trains them surely

اولادی که پدر و مادر نتوانست تربیت کند
روزگار تربیت خواهد کرد

- 235 -

From bit to bit one has much more
From piece to piece one fills the store

اندک اندک بهم شود بسیار، دانه دانه است غله در انبار

- 236 -

A thief is he, who steals the breeze
As he who from a mosque, a rug would seize

آن کس نسیم بدزدد دزد است،
آنکس گلیم از کعبه بدزدد دزد است

- 237 -

A charming face with a little pleasure
Is favored to the chest full of treasure

اندکی جمال به از بسیاری مال

- 238 -

In life the roles are differently played
Yet parts like this will also fade

این نیز بگذرد

- *239* -

The tail of a lion is in no way
A harmless toy for one to play

این دم شیر است ببازی مگیر

- *240* -

What a wise man can accomplish
A fool as well achieves
The fool, however will reach his goal
After damages that he leaves

آنچه دانا کند کند نادان،
لیک بعد از خرابی بسیار

- *241* -

His life's in total ruin
His high hopes are in vain
The odds are all against him
No breath left to complain

آه ندارد با ناله سودا کند

- 242 -

There's always peace
When war is ended
Disarm the troops
And differences are mended

آخر همه جنگی صلح است

. . . .

- 243 -

The one who's honest in the deal he makes
A share of the offered wealth he takes

آدم خوش معامله شریک مال مردم است

. . . .

- 244 -

What's past is past, do not regret
Think of the future better yet

افسوس گذشته را نباید خورد

. . . .

- *245* -

The hungry have no proper faith
Their will to pray is slight
The one obsession that they keep
Is to nurture themselves right

آدم گرسنه دین و ایمان درستی ندارد

. . . .

- *246* -

It may well be dollars
Or it may well be pound
Man is after money
Not the other way around

آدم پول را پیدا میکند، پول آدم را پیدا نمیکند

. . . .

- *247* -

He, who's alive, has the urge to live
A life so precious, that God did give

آدم زنده زندگی میخواهد

. . . .

- 248 -

One guest is sufficient for the host
To receive him gladly with a roast

اگر مهمان یکی باشد صاحب خانه برایش گاو میکشد

. . . .

- 249 -

If no one ever met their death
Humans would take each other's breath

اگر مردن نبود آدم آدم را میخورد

. . . .

- 250 -

If a prayer of a child
Had some effect
The life of a teacher
Would surely be wrecked

اگر دعای بچه اثر داشت، معلمی زنده نمی ماند

. . . .

- 251 -

To pick two watermelons with one hand
Is something unthinkable to understand

با یک دست دو هندوانه نمیتوان برداشت

- 252 -

Luck shows up just once you see
Grab it fast for it will flee

بخت یک بار خودش را بشما نشان میدهد

- 253 -

Greatness comes from being sage
Not from surplus of the age

بزرگی بعقل است نه بسال

- 254 -

His coat is full of pocket holes
His shoes are worn-out too
He limits his meal to once a day
And his rent is overdue
He can't afford to socialize
Much less to get a wife
Yet with these complexities
He's happy with his life

برهنه خوشحال است

- 255 -

There are forms of making fun
None of which amuses one

بریش کسی خندیدن

- 256 -

From the hand which gives
That hand receives
A fact that surely one believes

بهر دستی بدهی بهمان دست خواهی گرفت

- 257 -

He who never bothers
To toil or even strive
A life full of comfort
He'll likely not derive

— *Hafez*

براحتی نرسید آنکه زحمتی نکشید

. . . .

- 258 -

A faithful deed of a stranger
Is liable to make me related
While a friend whose kindness never was
to me will be so hated
Which indeed they forcibly take

بیگانه اگر وفا کند   خویش من است
ور دوست جفا کند بداندیش من است

. . . .

- 259 -

Man is a slave to affection
Kindness from others around
With all that love and caring
He will be heaven-bound

بشر بنده محبت است

. . . .

- 260 -

Who's your close friend
Tell me true
So I could picture the real you

بگو رفیقت کیست تا بگویم کیستی

. . . .

- 261 -

The bloom of a single flower
A springtime does not bring
However, the scent of each flower
Has the smell of the fabulous spring

با یک گل بهار نمیشود،
ولی هر گلی بوی بهار میدهد

. . . .

- 262 -

In the eye of the have ones
Life is certainly a beauty
Could it be that destiny
Is fulfilling its wondrous duty

بچشم بی نیازان زندگی زیباست

. . . .

- 263 -

He won't eat custard with the mighty king
For he places himself above everything

با شاه شله نمیخورد

· · · · · · · · · · · · · · · · · · ·

- 264 -

Does your tongue speak sweet and clearly
Or is your fortune worth dearly
Or are you close to me merely
If not, I'll abandon you sincerely

با زبان خوشت، با پول زیادت، با راه نزدیکت

· · · · · · · · · · · · · · · · · · ·

- 265 -

Those shiny cheeks of crimson
Present a brutal case
It's due to nothing other than
The slap that touched the face

با سیلی صورت خود را سرخ کردن

· · · · · · · · · · · · · · · · · · ·

- *266* -

It's plain and obvious we know why
Ladders do not lead us to the sky

با نردبان به آسمان نمیشود رفت

. . . .

- *267* -

They told him that his father
Had died from pure starvation
But he maintains that the poor deceased
Never touched his possession

باو گفتند بابات از گرسنگی مرد، گفت داشت، نخورد

. . . .

- *268* -

He who's well mannered
Will rule like a king
And he who has no manners
Will engage in anything

با ادب باش پادشاهی کن
بی ادب باش هر چه خواهی کن

. . . .

- 269 -

Frankly a fact that one can find
Is that the illiterate is totally blind

بیسواد کور است

. . . .

- 270 -

Putting one's foot into another one's shoe
Signifies the meddling that one can do

پا تو کفش دیگران کردن

. . . .

- 271 -

Prompt your mind, to make the truce
Regrets and worries have no use

پشیمانی سودی ندارد

. . . .

- 272 -

He wears his garment neatly
But his pocket's empty, completely

پز عالی، جیب خالی

. . . .

- 273 -

Respect the elderly people
Be warm to them, not bold
Continue to love them truthfully
Till you in turn are old

پیران را حرمت دار، تا به پیری برسی

. . . .

- 274 -

The eye of an ant
Has never been seen
Neither has the leg of a snake
Some clergy never break their bread
Which indeed they forcibly take

چشم مور و پای مار و نان ملا کسی ندیده

. . . .

- 275 -

Try to capture every heart
For breaking it, creates no art

تا توانی دلی بدست آور، دل شکستن هنر نمیباشد

. . . .

- 276 -

Fear be the brother of demise
When one becomes frightened
It's as though one dies

ترس برادر مرگ است

- 277 -

Until the well runs dry to naught
The value of water escapes one's thought

تا چاه خشک نشود قدر آب ندانی

- 278 -

Response to an idiot is keeping still
If not, then arguing he sure will

جواب ابلهان خاموشی است

- 279 -

Lines, spots and brows
Covering the world's face
Each item on this earth
Maintains its special place
— *Sheikh Mohammad Shabastari*

جهان چون خط و خال و چشم و ابروست،
که هر چیزی بجای خویش نیکوست

. . . .

- 280 -

The strike of God is soundless
Yet, it can't be endured
The blow is never groundless
And it is not to be cured

چوب خداوند صدا ندارد، وقتیکه زند دوا ندارد

. . . .

- 281 -

How can one come to explore
Who's out roaming beyond closed doors
Perhaps it's the merchant of a precious stone
Or a ragged peddler standing all alone

— Sa'di

چو در بسته باشد چه داند کسی،
که گوهر فروش است یا پیله ور

. . . .

- 282 -

I handed you a hatchet
Only to chop wood
But to tear down the sacred wall
I didn't say you could

ترا تیشه دادم که هیزم شکن
نگفتم که دیوار مسجد بکن

. . . .

Named after his grandfather 'The Sepahdar,' Iran's prime-minister in 1920, Fatollah Akbar was born in Tehran, Iran in 1940. He currently resides and works in the Washington, DC area. He is fluent in Persian, English, Russian, German and French.